I CAN BE A
TV CAMERA OPERATOR

By Kathryn Hallenstein

Prepared under the direction of Robert Hillerich, Ph.D.

CHILDRENS PRESS ™
CHICAGO

Library of Congress Cataloging in Publication Data

Hallenstein, Kathy.
  I can be a TV camera operator.

  Summary: Explains the work of the people who take
the pictures we see on television and offers some tips
on making this kind of work a career.
  1. Television camera operators—Vocational guidance
—Juvenile literature. [1. Television camera opeators
—Vocational guidance. 2. Vocational guidance.
3. Occupations] I. Title.   II. Title: TV camera
operator.
TR882.5.H35   1984   778.59'023   84-7665
ISBN 0-516-01842-6

PICTURE DICTIONARY

float

band

on location

parade

TV screen

sound person

light person

TV camera operator

crew

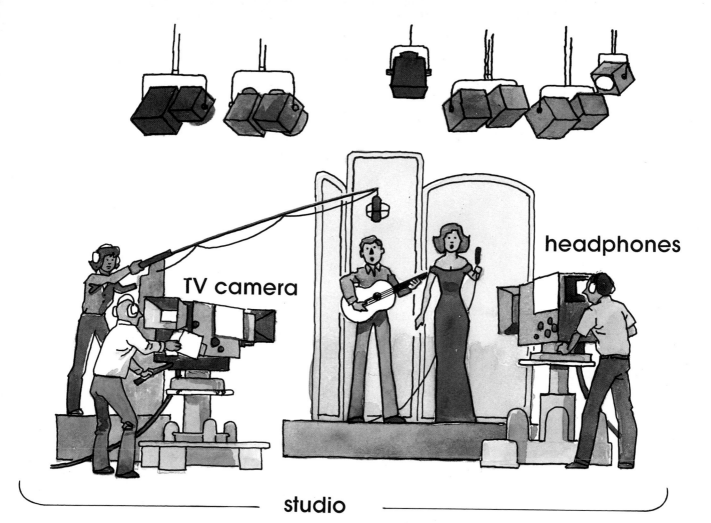

TV camera

headphones

studio

high school

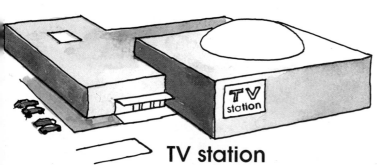

TV station

director

A TV camera operator uses a hand-held camera to take pictures at a ski race.

TV camera operators tell stories with pictures. They know what people want to see on their TV screens.

TV camera operator

TV camera operators take pictures on the ground (left) and from high places (right).
They show us as much of the parade as they can.

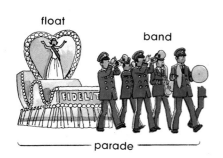

float

band

parade

When you watch a parade you want to see everything—the bands, the floats, the elephants, the people.

Camera operator at a football game

When you watch a ball game you want to follow the ball. TV camera operators know this. They know what to look for with their cameras.

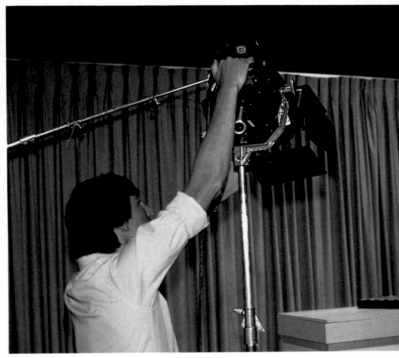

Light person

Director

Sound person

TV camera operators
work in teams called
crews. Each crew
member has a special
job. One person sets up
the lights. Another works
with the sound. The
director tells every crew
member what to· do.

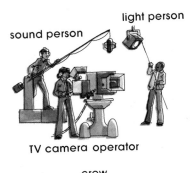

sound person

light person

TV camera operator

crew

director

Inside a TV studio

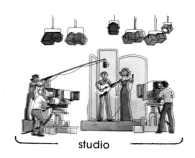

studio

Some TV camera operators work in a big room called a studio. Often, more than one camera is used in a studio.

Each camera has a number. The director tells each camera operator what pictures to take. The operators take pictures from different places in the studio. They take different pictures of the same thing.

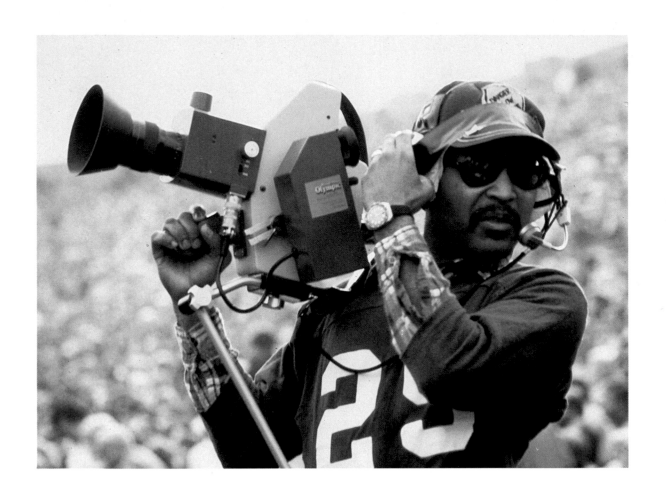

headphones

TV camera operators
wear headphones. The
director can talk to
each operator. The
director uses special
words.

The director looks at the pictures taken by different TV cameras and picks the shot he wants.

"Shoot" means to take
a picture.
"Zoom in" means to
get a close-up shot.
"Pan" means to move
the camera slowly.

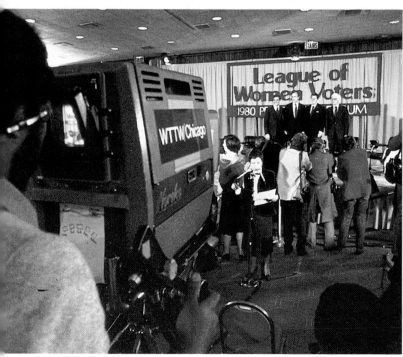

TV cameras can move in many different directions.

While working, TV camera operators are always busy. They must watch the action through the cameras. They must listen to the director's orders. They must be ready to move their cameras up and down, left and right, forward and backward.

TV camera operators
also work outside.
Working outside the
studio is called going
"on location."

on location

On location, TV
camera operators often
use smaller cameras.

A crew may go on
location to a fire. They
may go to cover a big
snow storm.

TV camera operators
must be fast. Sometimes
there may be only one

chance to get a good
shot. Camera operators
must always be
watching and thinking.
Their cameras must be
in the right place at the
right time.

TV camera operators must know what to put in a picture. They must know what is important and what is not important. This is called "framing the shot."

Look at these pictures. Which TV camera operator has done the best job of "framing a shot"?

How do you learn to be a TV camera operator?

First you must finish high school. Then you may apply for a job at a TV station. Many people want to be TV camera operators. TV stations will pick only the best people for the job. To be the best you must study and learn as much as you can.

high school

TV station

Some TV camera operators go to school to learn to take pictures.

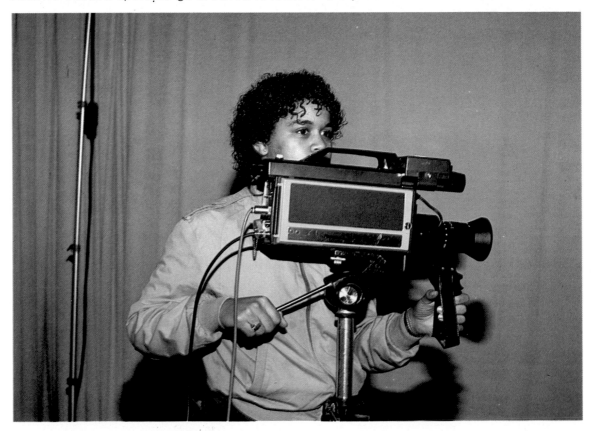

Some TV camera
operators learn their job
at a TV station. Others
go to school to learn
how to use a camera.

Would you like to be a TV camera operator? You can if you learn the right things.

You must learn to listen and follow directions. You must learn to work well with other people.

You must learn how to "frame a shot." TV camera operators know what people want to see on their TV screens.

TV camera operators work in cold weather. They work in hot weather. Sometimes they work during the day. At other times they work at night.

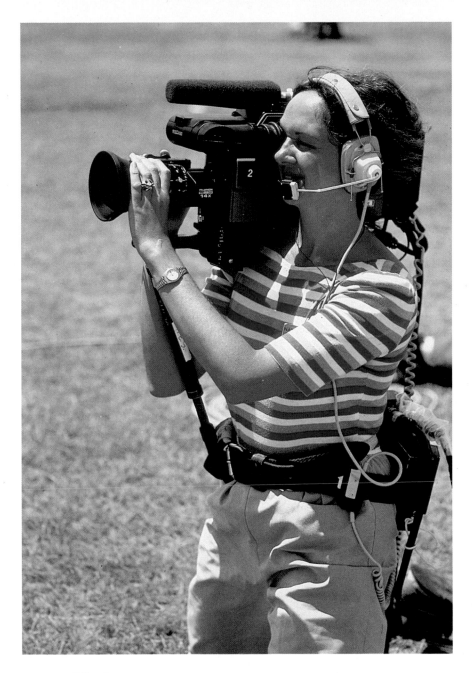

TV camera operators
work hard to make the
TV shows we watch.

WORDS YOU SHOULD KNOW

action (AK • shun)—what is going on

apply (uh • PLY)—to ask for a job

backward (BAK • werd)—toward the back

camera (KAM • er • uh)—a machine for taking pictures

crew (KROO)—a group of people working together

director (di • REK • ter)—a person who decides how things should be done and tells others what to do

float (FLOHT)—a large, flat car that is made to look beautiful for a parade

forward (FOR • werd)—toward the front

framing (FRAYM • ing)—taking a picture so that it best shows what is important

headphones (HED • fohnz)—telephone earpieces that are held to the head by a band

location (loh • KAY • shun)—a place outside a studio where camera operators are sent to take pictures of what is happening

member (MEM • ber)—a person, an animal, or a thing that belongs to a group

operator (AHP • uh • ray • ter)—a person who runs a machine, a telephone, or a business

screen (SKREEN)—the part of the TV where the pictures appear

studio (STOO • dee • oh)—the place where TV shows are made and sent out

study (STUD • ee)—to try to learn by reading and thinking

zoom (ZOOM)—to make something look nearer or farther away

INDEX

PHOTO CREDITS

©Ken May—8 (top right), 18

Hillstrom Stock Photos: © Ray F. Hillstrom—5, 19 (left); © Jon Randolph—14 (top); © Don and Pat Valenti—4, 14 (bottom right); © David R. Frazier—19 (right)

© Jon Randolph—6 (left), 8 (top left), 14 (bottom left), 20 (2 photos)

© Sister Tecla Jaehnen—24 (2 photos)

© James Mejuto—Cover, 22, 26, 28

Nawrocki Stock Photo: © Harvey Moshman—6 (right), 8 (bottom), 10, 13; © Candee—7, 12

Tom Stack & Associates: © Tom Stack—28 (top); © Brian Parker—29

© M. Messenger—16

© Cindy Van Vreede—25

Cover—CBS TV camera operator at Gulf Classic

ABOUT THE AUTHOR

Kathryn Hallenstein started out as a special education teacher in San Diego, California. She returned to her hometown of Chicago and entered the publishing field in 1977. Since that time she has developed numerous games, puzzles, books, videotapes, and filmstrips for children in elementary grades.

Ms. Hallenstein is currently working on educational microcomputer software and living in a suburb of Chicago with her daughter, Natalie.